MW01530516

TABLE OF CONTENTS

Cover Art by
Matthew Archambault

Black & White Illustrations by
Ken Landgraf

EDCON
Publishing Group

Copyright © 2006
AV Concepts Corporation
Edcon Publishing Group

Find More Products Like this at:
www.rempub.com
1-800-826-4740

Printed in U.S.A.
ISBN# 1-55576-386-3

RECOGNIZING DEPRESSION PART I

Learning About Depression

The BLAHS

The BLUES

and ROTTEN MOODS

WHAT TEENS SHOULD **KNOW** ABOUT DEPRESSION

How's life treating you these days? Blue skies and happiness? Or are you on the down side? You know, down in the dumps?

It's normal to have good moods and bad moods. It's not unusual at all to have

feelings of happiness

suddenly turn to sadness.

Have you ever gone to school expecting to have a good day, only to have your expectations ruined by an argument with a friend?. . .

Or a failing grade?

Sure you have!

Think about how you would feel if the following happened to you:

"Betty, it's not enough that you failed another English test, now I find out that you just got detention for not cleaning out your locker."

"I'm sorry, Albert, I want to break up with you. I don't want to see you anymore."

Hey, it's not the end of the world you tell yourself. There are lots of fish in the sea. But, you still have to admit that you still have a little bit of the blahs.

On the other hand, think about how you would feel in the following situations:

"Sure. You can use the car tonight and, by the way, I'm raising your allowance," said Dad.

"Helen, will you go to the Dance with me Saturday night? You will? That's great! My dad is going to let me use the car. How about I pick you up at 7:30? Okay, great. I'll see you then. Bye."

Your feelings in these situations are much different, aren't they?

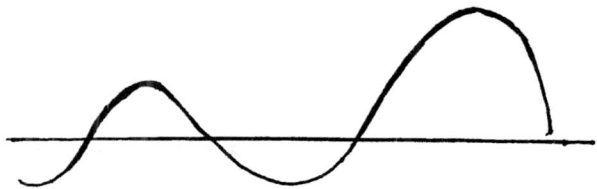

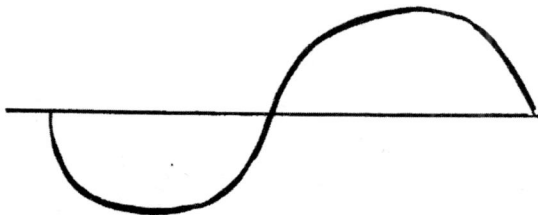

Most of us have cycles. Sometimes we're happy. Sometimes we're sad. Whenever you experience a low cycle, what do you call it? Maybe you say,

"I'VE GOT
THE
BLAHS"

or perhaps it's

"THE BLUES"

or it could be that you're just in

"A ROTTEN MOOD"

Whatever you call it, most of the time things seem to balance out. On the other hand, some people experience sadness that just won't go away. This kind of sadness is referred to as

DEPRESSION

Depression is an emotional imbalance that has many symptoms that occur over a long period of time and just won't go away – no matter how much you try to overcome them.

> **HEALTH:**
> *Physical*
> *Emotional*
> *Spiritual*
> *Mental*

Symptoms of depression interfere with a person's ability to function in a healthy way. They interfere in the areas of *physical, emotional, spiritual,* and *mental* health.

Depression in healthy people usually occurs along with a sad event. This sadness passes within a few days or weeks.
In more serious depression, nothing seems to bring relief from the sadness . . .

not even happy events!

It's not typical for people to be in a good mood and to be happy ALL the time.

People who are happy all the time may be masking the disease of depression.

Personal Development

Also, it's not a good sign to be sad all the time. Feeling "down-in-the-dumps" much of the time is a more obvious indicator of depression.

SADNESS

Sadness is a sign of depression.

"No one cares about me anyhow. Why should I care about anyone."

LONELINESS

Loneliness, or a sense of being alone, is another sign of depression.

A change in your appetite — either an unexplained loss or an increase — is a possible indicator of depression.

"Who can think of food when their whole life seems a waste?"

"Who cares about fat? I'm so fat now, it doesn't matter. I'm just going to have one more ice-cream cone."

ANXIOUS

"It's no use. It's just never going to work. I should have never tried."

Personal
Development

IRRITABLE

"It just makes me so mad. Now, what's going to happen? The coach will probably kick me off the team. I'll be the laughing stock of the school. Why can't people just leave me alone?"

Mike looks angry, and anger can be a symptom of depression. This is particularly true if someone overreacts to the least provocation.

"Just leave me alone. I told you – I don't want to go to that movie. Get lost!"

Teenagers who take unnecessary risks, like crossing the railroad tracks when the warning gate is down, or repeatedly act without thinking about the consequences of their behavior, may be depressed.

If you find that you're quick to anger every time things don't go your way – or you act without thinking and are on the edge all the time, expecting everything to go wrong – these might be signs of depression.

Sometimes depression can be simple and brief. For instance, if someone close to you dies.

REACTIVE

DEPRESSION

You will experience grief and a depressed reaction to the death. This is an example of REACTIVE DEPRESSION.

CHRONIC

ACUTE

ACUTE DEPRESSION is brief and generally lasts less than six months. If the depressed state lasts for more than six months, then it is called CHRONIC DEPRESSION.

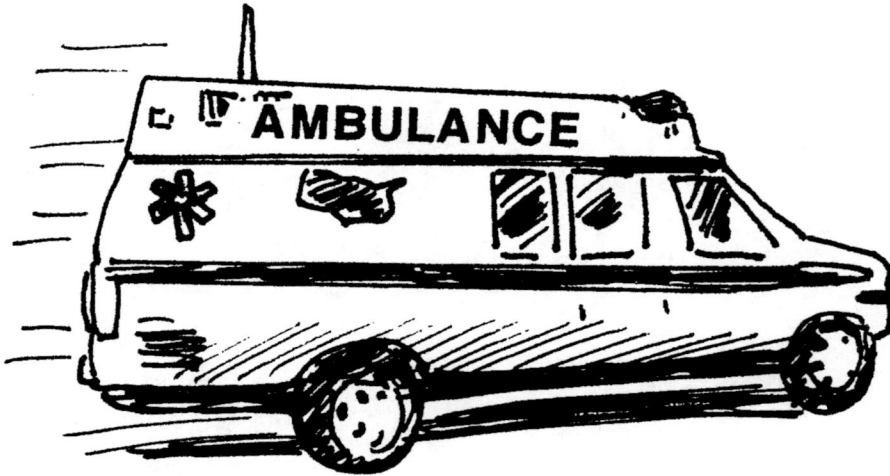

The chronically depressed person may not be able to control the symptoms. This kind of depression is more likely than reactive depression to be life threatening. In fact, suicide is occasionally a tragic ending to the life of a chronically depressed person.

Now, let's review some of the symptoms of depression in teens:

1. **Sadness and Moodiness**
2. **Loneliness**
3. **Changes in Appetite**
4. **Anxiety & Irritability**
5. **Anger & Impulsiveness**
6. **Change in Sleep Habits**
7. **Self-defeating & Suicidal Thoughts**
8. **Hopelessness**
9. **Decrease in Ability to Function**

Personal Development

Other signs of depression might be the withdrawal from family or friends,

persistent boredom or a decline in schoolwork,

rebellious or violent behavior,

drug or alcohol abuse,

neglect of appearance and lack of personal hygiene, or any sudden change in personality.

It's important to recognize the danger signs of depression in a friend. Learn to recognize the symptoms early on.

There are teens who manifest "covert" depression. (Everyone has heard of the "super-kid" – the model student who suddenly kills him or herself.) Teens who manifest COVERT DEPRESSION appear to have it "all together." When you ask them how things are going, they'll always say, "fine."

Just because a teen "has it all together" on the *outside*, doesn't mean that life is all that great.

If you are one of those kids, who do you turn to for help? Who can you trust? Who's going to keep it a secret?

Recognizing depression is only the beginning. Our next step is doing something about it.

RECOGNIZING DEPRESSION
PART I

Learning About Depression

1. How would you describe the blahs? ______________________

____

____

____

____

____

2. What is the difference between feeling the blahs and depression?

____

____

____

____

____

3. How would you explain "covert" depression? ______________

____

____

____

____

____

TRUE (T) or FALSE (F)

_____ 1. It is normal to have good moods and bad moods.

_____ 2. Depression is a feeling of sadness that won't go away.

_____ 3. Having an argument with a friend will cause serious depression in a healthy person.

_____ 4. A change in one's appetite is a definite sign of depression.

_____ 5. Sleeping too much or too little can be a signal of depression.

_____ 6. Acute depression lasts a brief time (less than 6 months).

_____ 7. Chronic depression lasts 6 months or more.

_____ 8. The symptoms of chronic depression are easily controlled.

_____ 9. Anger is not a sign of depression.

_____ 10. Reactive depression usually leads to suicide.

Answers can be found on page 40.

EDCON PUBLISHING

Personal Development

Learning About Depression

FILL IN THE BLANKS
Fill in the blanks with the words from the box below.

personality	sad	anger	recovery	normal
sadness	suicide	relief	loneliness	neglect

1. Depression interferes with one's ability to function in a
    _____ way.

2. Depression in healthy people usually occurs along with a
    _____ event.

3. In serious depression, nothing seems to bring
    _____; not even happy events.

4. _____, _____, and _____ are
    all symptoms of depression.

5. Occasionally, a chronically depressed person is capable of
    _____.

6. A sudden change in _____ is a signal that
    someone may be depressed.

7. _____ of appearance and personal hygiene may be
    symptoms of depression.

8. Recognizing depression is the first step toward
    _____.

Answers can be found on page 40.

RECOGNIZING DEPRESSION PART II

EDCON PUBLISHING

Personal Development

WHAT TO DO ABOUT DEPRESSION

"Jeff, are you in there?" asked Megan. "Why are you sitting alone in this dark room?"

"Go away, Megan," Jeff said angrily. "I don't want to talk to anyone. Everything is going wrong!"

Megan switched on the light. Jeff quickly covered his eyes with his hands.

"Jeff, please talk to me about what's bothering you. You scare me when you sound angry. And your mom said you didn't eat supper."

50,000,000

Megan is right to be concerned, because Jeff has at least two symptoms of depression. There are fifty-million people who suffer from depression.

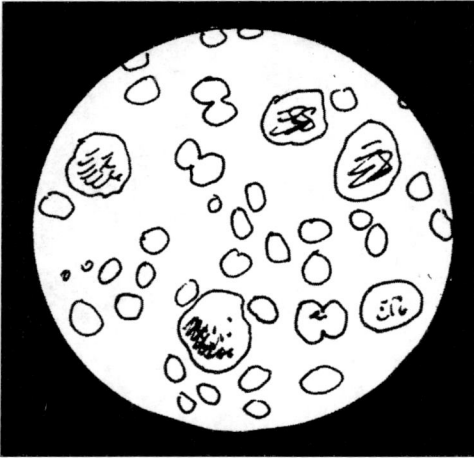

Depression is called the "common cold" of mental illness. It's a disease, and it's treatable.

"Well, Megan," said Jeff, "I've been feeling rotten since you and I broke up. I thought we would be together forever."

Megan answered, "Jeff, since we were both going to be so far apart from each other in college, we agreed that we shouldn't go steady. You seemed sure of it last week. What happened?"

26

"Getting that football scholarship means a lot," said Jeff. "And now I'm not sure I will get it after yesterday's game."

Jeff went on, "Mom and Dad argue constantly about money – and college costs may break up their marriage." He continued, "And I'm sick of sharing a room with my brother, and now – you and I . . ."

27

Jeff feels like he's at the end of his rope.

He's vulnerable.

VULNERABLE

Such combined conditions — and grief — can cause depression but, for most of us, it's temporary, and will soon pass.

If such feelings remain with us, then the situation becomes more serious. It is a chronic depression and must be treated with counseling and, possibly, medicine.
Coupled with severe stress, depression can be fatal.
Depressed individuals often feel trapped.

EDCON PUBLISHING

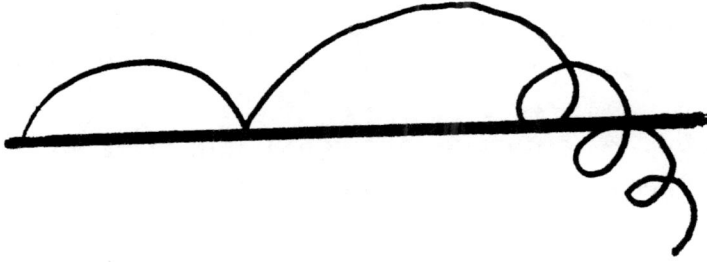

Loneliness, despair, hopelessness and helplessness spiraling ever downward is chronic depression – and can lead to suicidal thoughts.

Individuals who are chronically depressed often send signals. They become more withdrawn. Their thoughts, writings and language often become preoccupied with themes about death and dying. Their behavior is reckless with an indifference to the consequences.

Then grades drop. They sabotage long-term friendships, and they become highly critical of themselves, sometimes turning to drugs or alcohol. They often begin to give away their possessions.

"Jeff, you surprise me," said Megan. "Last week you said that everything was fine. I don't think I can handle this change."

"I'd like to talk to someone," answered Jeff. "But, who? I don't want the world to know my thoughts. Everyone would just talk about me."

"If you really want to talk to someone," said Megan, "why not make an appointment with Mrs. Butler, the school's counselor. She's a professional counselor and keeps everything you say, confidential. She won't tell anybody if you don't want her to."

EDCON PUBLISHING

That's good advice. Counselors are protected by law from revealing confidential information. This is called PRIVILEDGED COMMUNICATION.

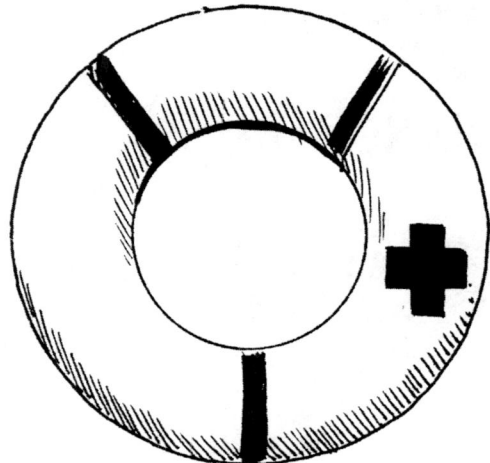

Most professionals are obliged by law to preserve life, even if that means breaking a confidence – but, this seldom happens.

In fact, it reduces some of the pressure on teens and lets them know that the counselor is taking their verbalizations seriously.

TEEN PRESSURE COOKER

Those problems that seem unmanageable can be resolved with help. REACH OUT!

EDCON PUBLISHING

There are people whose lives are dedicated to helping. It's not only their livelihood, it's their life's work. You are only a call away from help.

"I really feel embarrassed about talking to anyone," Jeff went on. "Besides, no one else is suffering the way that I am."

"You're right," said Megan. "No one can feel exactly the way you do because we are all different people. But, Jeff, give others a chance to help. It isn't your fault if this feeling doesn't go away."

                    *   *   *

Jeff should make an appointment to see a counselor, a minister, a priest, or a rabbi. There are many organizations to turn to for help. The trained professionals will help you without scolding or reprimanding you.
There are loving, caring individuals who will help you solve your problems. Where do you find such organizations?

Look in the telephone book under MENTAL HEALTH.

CRISIS LINE
1-888-000-0000

Every city has a Crisis Line for people reaching out for help.

CONTACT

There's a telephone call-in service called CONTACT.

SUICIDE
HOTLINE

There are Suicide Hotlines.

Most communities have MENTAL HEALTH CENTERS nearby. Or you can call them for help.

Most of these organizations will not involve family if you don't want them to – except to preserve your life. Everything is confidential – it's kept secret. It doesn't matter if you're rich or poor, an "A" student or average, you are a human being – and a valuable person.

Remember, depression is a rather common problem in the teenage years – lots of mood swings – lots of pressures to grow, change and achieve.

EDCON PUBLISHING

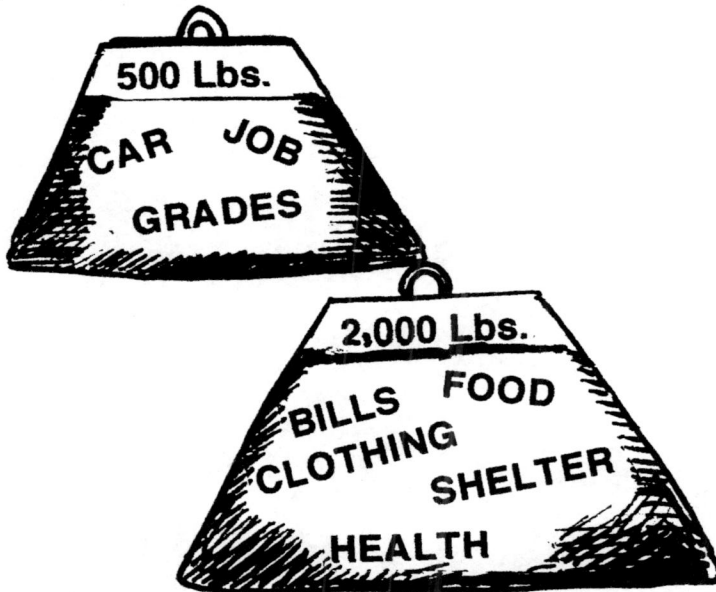

500 Lbs.
CAR JOB GRADES

2,000 Lbs.
BILLS FOOD
CLOTHING SHELTER
HEALTH

Adults don't have the same kinds of pressures teens have. That's why it's sometimes hard for teens to talk to adults – it's difficult to get them to understand.

"Jeff, there's no shame in being depressed," said Megan. "It takes courage and strength to face your problems. If you are feeling desperate, as I know that you are, then you have to get some help from others.

"I can tell you what I do when I'm feeling low. I make mental pictures and say, 'This will pass. Tomorrow the sun will rise and life will go on. Time will heal my hurts.'

"Marybeth says that prayer helps her. She says her religion forbids suicide, but that it sure helps her with depression."

"Megan, I know suicide is taboo," answered Jeff. "That's what stops me. With suicide there is no tomorrow. It's so final.

"But, I still have hope. Just talking to you has helped."

"I'm not enough, Jeff," answered Megan. "I wish you would talk to your teacher or the school's counselor, or share this with your buddy, Bill."

"I might talk to coach Jackson," said Jeff.

"Or maybe my grand-dad will go fishing with me."

Call For Help

See, you CAN think of some-body to talk to if you work on it. If you can make one call, you can get help for your depression.

You Are Not Alone

If you can think of one person, then you are not alone. You CAN get rid of your blues and enjoy a full, happy life.

Personal Development

WHAT TO DO ABOUT DEPRESSION

FILL IN THE BLANKS
Fill in the blanks with the words from the box below.

rabbis	chronic	scold
trust	drugs	confide
priests	death	alcohol
reprimand	dying	medicine
ministers	reveal	counseling
withdrawn	fatal	possessions

1. A serious form of depression is called _____

    depression.

2. Persons who are chronically depressed are often

    _____. They tend to talk about

    _____ and _____.

3. The chronically depressed individual often turns to

    _____ or _____.

4. Severely depressed persons who begin to give away their

    _____ need immediate help!

5. Coupled with severe stress, depression can be

    _____.

WHAT TO DO ABOUT DEPRESSION

FILL IN THE BLANKS
Fill in the blanks with the words from the box below.

rabbis	chronic	scold
trust	drugs	confide
priests	death	alcohol
reprimand	dying	medicine
ministers	reveal	counseling
withdrawn	fatal	possessions

6. Depression may be treated with _____ and,

sometimes, _____.

7. Find someone to talk with – someone you can

_____ and _____ in.

8. Counselors, by law, may not _____ your

confidence against your wishes, except to preserve life.

9. _____, _____, and _____ are

trained to counsel those in need of help.

10. Trained professionals will not _____ or

_____ you.

Answers can be found on page 40.

WHAT TO DO ABOUT DEPRESSION

TRUE (T) or FALSE (F)

_____1. Depression is never fatal.

_____2. 50,000,000 people suffer from depresssion.

_____3. Depression is a treatable disease.

_____4. No one wants to associate with a depressed person, therefore, it is difficult to obtain counseling.

_____5. The telephone book is a good source of organizations that can help the depressed person.

_____6. Every city has a Crisis Line for those reaching out for help.

_____7. The Suicide Hotline offers assistance only to those persons who have tried to take their life.

_____8. Your local Mental Health Clinic is equipped with professionals who can assist the depressed person seeking recovery.

_____9. Depressed persons do not have to face their problems alone; there is help available for anyone in need.

Answers can be found on page 40.

ANSWER KEY

RECOGNIZING DEPRESSION, PART I

TRUE or FALSE

1.	T	6.	T
2.	T	7.	T
3.	F	8.	F
4.	F	9.	F
5.	T	10.	F

FILL IN THE BLANKS

1. normal
2. sad
3. relief
4. Loneliness, sadness, anger (in any order)
5. suicide
6. personality
7. Neglect
8. recovery

RECOGNIZING DEPRESSION, PART II

FILL IN THE BLANKS   TRUE or FALSE

1. chronic	1.	F
2. withdrawn, death, dying	2.	T
3. drugs, alcohol	3.	T
4. possessions	4.	F
5. fatal	5.	T
6. counseling, medicine	6.	T
7. trust, confide	7.	F
8. reveal	8.	T
9. Ministers, priests, rabbis (in any order)	9.	T
10. scold, reprimand		